# A Very Young Circus Flyer

**Also by Jill Krementz**

*The Face of South Vietnam*
(with text by Dean Brelis)

*Sweet Pea—A Black Girl
Growing Up in the Rural South*

*Words and Their Masters*
(with text by Israel Shenker)

*A Very Young Dancer*

*A Very Young Rider*

*A Very Young Gymnast*

# A Very Young Circus Flyer

Written and Photographed by

## Jill Krementz

Alfred A. Knopf, New York, 1979

This is a Borzoi Book
published by Alfred A. Knopf, Inc.
Copyright © 1979 by Jill Krementz
All rights reserved under International and Pan-American Copyright Conventions.
Published in the United States by Alfred A. Knopf, Inc., New York, and
simultaneously in Canada by Random House of Canada Limited, Toronto.
Distributed by Random House, Inc., New York.

Library of Congress Cataloging in Publication Data
Krementz, Jill.
A very young circus flyer.
1. Farfan, Armando—Juvenile literature.
2. Aerialists—Biography—Juvenile literature.
[1. Aerialists.   2. Circus]   I. Title.
GV1811.F34K73      791.3'4'0924    [B]    78-20546
ISBN 0-394-50574-3

Manufactured in the United States of America
Published March 28, 1979
Second Printing, April 1979

*I first photographed the circus in 1964 for the
New York Herald Tribune. Ben Price was the picture
editor of that newspaper, and it was he who hired me as a
staff photographer. This book is dedicated to him —
with my thanks and with love.*

*—J.K.*

I really love the circus. I've lived with it ever since I was born, but I've only been working for two years. I'm a trapeze artist with Ringling Bros. and Barnum & Bailey. I learned to fly when I was four. I'm nine now. My official name is Armando Farfan, Jr., but everyone calls me Tato. My whole family flies together and we're called the Flying Farfans.

My mother is from Czechoslovakia, where her parents owned a circus. Her grandparents and her great-grandparents also owned a circus. In addition to flying with us, Mama has a dog act in the first half of the show called Miss Anna's Oodles of Poodles. And she has a lot of Dobermans she's training for next year.

My father, Armando, is the catcher in our flying act. He's from Chile. His family had a circus for a long time too, but they lost it in a hurricane in Nicaragua. I call him Poppy because the Spanish word for papa is *popito*. He's hoping to have his own circus someday.

My parents have been with Ringling for four years. Before that they were with lots of circuses in Europe and in the United States. In 1976 they won the circus "Oscar" in Monaco. It's made of pure silver.

My brother Gino is fourteen, and he's just learned a 3½, which makes him the youngest flyer ever to accomplish this. He got a special diploma from the Circus Society. A 3½ is when you do three and a half somersaults in the air before the catcher grabs your ankles. If you fall into the net, it's still called a 3½ but it doesn't count. Gino is hoping to be the first person to do a quadruple. I'm going to have a hard time keeping up with him. Right now I'm catching a double and working on a triple.

When Gino isn't flying, he likes to ride his motorcycle. He lets me ride it too.

I live on the circus train, which is painted silver. There are about twenty-five cars for people to live in, and lots more called flat cars and stock cars for holding the circus wagons and the elephants when we travel. And there's the pie car. That's what we call the place where we can go and eat. It's like a restaurant but only circus people get to go there.

When the train isn't moving, I like to swing and play on it.

Wherever we're parked, that's our backyard. I love to play soccer with my Dad and Gino. Poppy was a famous soccer player. He used to own a soccer team, and his team was Nevada State Champion. We have a whole shelf of trophies.

We live in Car Number 41. It's just like living in a mobile home. We have curtains, wallpaper, wall-to-wall red shag carpeting, and air conditioning. There's a bedroom for my parents, with a double bed, and we have our own bathroom. We spend most of our time in the main room, which is about 38 feet long. It's like a big living room with a dining area where we eat and where Gino and I do our homework. At night my brother and I sleep in a big bed, which pulls out over the dining-room table.

We have a TV but it gets a little blurry when the train is moving. I like watching the cartoons the best, especially Mighty Mouse.

We've had a fish tank for over a year. We started out with eighteen goldfish, but when the train moves they get sick so we have only seven left. While we're traveling, my Dad puts a rope around the tank and a plastic bag on the top with lots of towels to keep the water in. When we first got the tank, everyone thought we were crazy. They still do.

We also have some puppies because one of Mom's Dobermans named Cricket just had four of them in the closet. We gave two of them away, and I called the ones we kept Susie and Pino.

Every year around Christmas time the show rehearses for a month in Venice, Florida. We get our new acts into shape and rehearse the production numbers for the year coming up. Tim Holst is the performance director, and he makes sure everything runs smoothly.

The choreographer shows us how to position ourselves and where to walk. He keeps reminding us to smile at the audience—to make them feel that they're part of the circus.

The ringmaster is one of the most important people in the show because he announces the acts and keeps everything moving. He blows his whistle to begin and finish every act, and he also cues the orchestra.

Everyone has to practice walking around the track, even the animals. There are three production numbers that all the performers and animals have to be in—the opening and closing marches, and the Spectacle, which is just before intermission and has a different theme every two years.

Dwayne Cunningham, one of the clowns, didn't find walking all that easy. He kept talking to his donkey, saying, "Come on, Jennie.... If you want to be in show business, you'll have to learn to walk around the track one whole time without stopping."

John Russell had a hard time too. His stilts are 10 feet high, and it took him three months to learn how to walk on them. In the beginning he just leaned against a wall and moved along beside it.

While we're rehearsing, the Felds, who are the producers of the show, drop in and watch us. One time there was a girl I didn't know—she turned out to be a big doll that the clowns use in one of their acts.

This year Mom is going to ride Ronnie, the lead elephant, in Spec, so she had to learn how to get up on her and, even more important, how to *stay* on. Gunther Gebel-Williams, who is the star of the whole show and in charge of all the animals, gave her a lesson.

The hardest thing about riding an elephant is getting on. You stand on its left foot and grab its ear with your right hand, and with your left hand you grab its headpiece. Then the elephant tosses you up.

Mama said it made her legs sore. That's because you have to press your legs hard against the elephant's back to keep from falling off.

Poppy rides a stallion, but he did that last year too, so all he had to do this year was practice.

Don Foote designs the costumes for the production numbers. He measures me once a year to see if I've grown. This year I grew 2 inches taller and my waist grew half an inch. My Dad is hoping I'll stay small, to make it easier for him to catch me.

Don even designs costumes for the elephants, horses, camels, and monkeys. The tigers and lions don't wear costumes. He likes dressing the clowns and elephants best. He uses thousands of feathers and millions of sequins. He told me that if you put all the sequins in a row, they would measure about twenty miles.

The performers have to supply the costumes for their own acts, and Mama and Poppy make ours. We wear leotards decorated with pretty colors and lots of rhinestones for our flying act. They're called leotards because the flying trapeze was invented about a hundred years ago by a Frenchman named Jules Léotard. Mama also makes her own costume for her poodle act. She goes to a special feather factory in Philadelphia every two years to get lots of pink feathers for it.

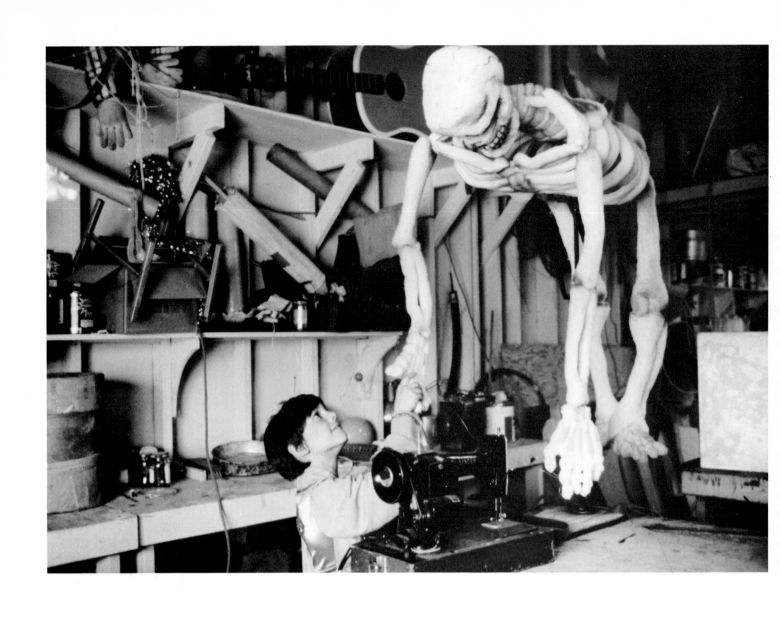

I love the clown workshop where the clowns make the props for their gags. It looks like Toyland.

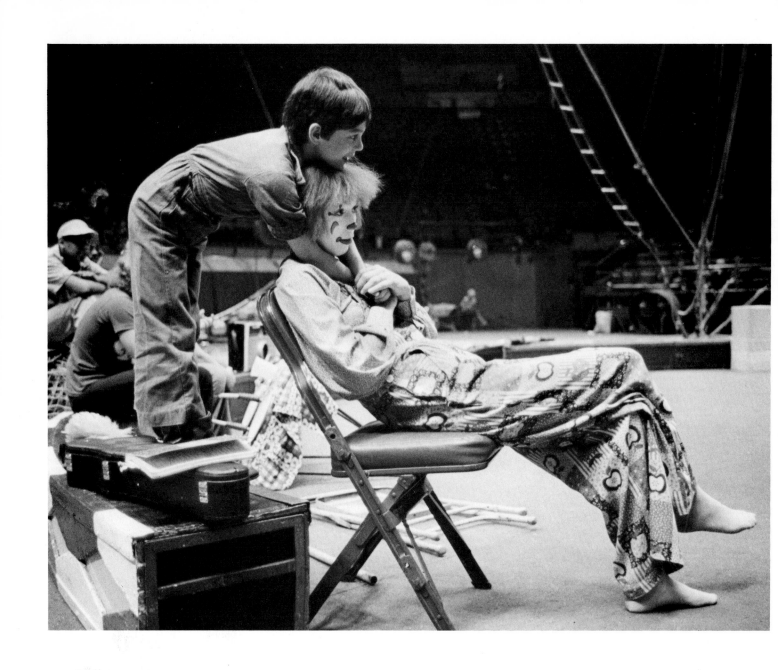

When we're not working on the big production numbers or getting our costumes ready, we all have to work on our new acts. I like to watch the clowns practice their gags. There's a special Clown College where they teach you slaps and falls. And they even have courses on how to make false noses and how to walk in big floppy shoes.

Gunther is from Germany, and he's been working with animals since he was twelve. Some people think that his tigers, pumas, leopards, and panthers have been de-clawed and have had their teeth taken out, but it isn't true. One time Gunther had to have forty stitches in his arm because one of the cats bit him. And he's luckier than some of his friends. Since 1900, twenty-one trainers have been killed in the circus arena.

He got his tigers when they were little babies, and his wife fed them with a bottle for weeks. Now they eat raw meat and Gunther feeds them himself. He says it gives him more control over them in the ring.

The first thing a big cat has to learn is how to step on to a pedestal and stay there until it's told to move.

Gunther also has an act of liberty horses. He brought the horses with him when he came from Europe. He got them in Yugoslavia. When he's practicing, he uses a lunge line, but during the show he depends on his voice alone.

People call him the Lord of the Ring. Sometimes people call him an animal tamer, but he says that's wrong. Wild beasts can only be *trained*. They can never be tamed.

I don't get to watch the other acts as much as I'd like to because we have to work most of the time on our flying act. My Dad supervises everything that has to do with the flying trapeze.

The safety net is made out of Dacron, and it's about 13 feet wide when stretched. There's a section at each end called the apron, and that's about 2 feet wider just to make it safer. People always ask me if I fly without a net, and the answer to that is "No!" Léotard used a long mattress, but every flyer after him has used a net. You'd have to be crazy not to use one.

We use two bars in our act: the catch bar for Poppy, and the fly bar for Mom, Gino, and me. The bars are made of steel, and they'll bend but they'll never break.

Before I go up, my Dad usually makes me sit down and *think* about what I'm going to do. First I learn my timing. Then I learn how to control my distance in order to be catchable. Then I work on getting enough height to my swing. The last thing is to make my wrists stiff enough so the catcher can catch me. That's the hardest part for me. I have marks all over my hands where Poppy catches me but can't hold on because my wrists are too loose.

The most important thing, though, is my concentration.

I climb up a rope ladder to the platform, which is about 32 feet high. I grab on to the bar and take a few practice swings. The first swing has to be easy and slow so I don't pull any muscles. My father is always telling me: "Keep your knees together and don't bend them. Don't look like a frog. Even if you fall, I want your knees together."

I like swinging the best because it's so easy. I'm not likely to mess up and go to the net.

Whenever I make a new trick and catch it for the first time, my father gives me a kiss...like Burt Lancaster did to Gina Lollobrigida in the movie *Trapeze*. All circus people know that movie.

And every time I miss, I go to the net. Running on the net is much harder than it looks. But it's a lot more exciting than walking, because you get to bounce up and down.

When I start to learn a new trick, I use a safety rope, which is called a mechanic. One end of the rope is attached to a belt around my waist, and the other end is controlled by Mama, who's standing below on the ground. That's so I won't hurt myself, because even though there's a net it doesn't help if you fall the wrong way.

When I miss, my Dad gets so angry—especially when I do something wrong or dangerous that might make me get hurt. He always says: "Son, I've told you a thousand times—do I have to repeat myself? *You're* supposed to be doing the work. I'm only supposed to catch you. Throw your legs up. And get more height. The higher you jump, the easier it is to make your trick."

Luckily for us, Poppy gets dizzy after more than an hour and a half upside down, so then we get to stop.

After everyone is finished working out, it's fun to play on the web. That's what the showgirls work on. I make believe that I'm Spider-Man.

Then Poppy and Gino roll up the net and put it away to give other performers room to practice. The net weighs about 150 pounds.

We usually make videotapes of our practice sessions and study them afterwards. If we watch them in slow motion, we can see our mistakes.

We also work on my Mom's dog act. Gino and I are in charge of bringing the dogs from our trailer to the ring.

Mama has four standard poodles and two miniature ones. They all have short names because it's easier to talk to them that way.

We started training the dogs when they were eight months old. When they're younger than that, they can't concentrate. Neither could I.

Before we leave Florida, the dogs get a bath and then they get dyed pink. Mama sprays them with red food coloring mixed with water. Then she clips them so they'll look real fancy.

All the animals in the show get a complete checkup from Doc Henderson, the Ringling vet. He's been with Ringling since 1941. His patients include elephants, tigers, leopards, pumas, llamas, donkeys, horses, ponies, chimps, and dogs. Sometimes if I get a sore throat he takes care of me too. He's always saying that he'd rather dance with a tiger than with a chimp. The chimps are really mean.

When we're in winter headquarters, we just have to rehearse from nine to five and then we're free. It's about the only time we get to go out at night and do things, because after the season starts we have so many evening shows. I really like playing table soccer and billiards. But the pinball machines are what I love best.

On our last day in Florida we have a dress rehearsal, and then it's time to take the show on the road. We pack our wardrobe trunks, the trains are loaded, and we're off to the first town.

We leave at night, so I usually go right to bed, but during the day it's fun to wave to people from the vestibule. We travel about 15,000 miles a year, and last year we visited fifty-two cities.

As soon as we get to a town where we're performing, the animals are unloaded, because there are more comfortable places for them to stay than on the train. They have special stabling areas, either in the building where we're performing or in tents nearby.

Oliver Gebel-Williams helps his father unload the elephants. Then there's usually a parade of all the animals through the streets.

The elephants are always such show-offs!

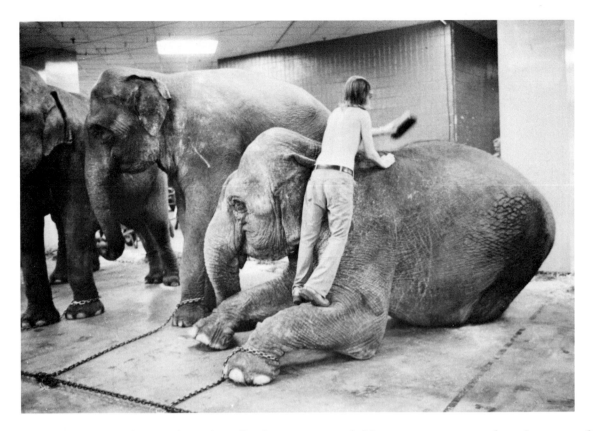

As soon as the animals arrive in their new stabling quarters, they're washed and fed. Sometimes the elephants get vegetable-oil facials if their skin is too dry, or pedicures if they have hangnails. Gunther and his men take care of all the animals.

An elephant weighs between 4 and 5 tons and drinks about 30 or 40 gallons of water a day. They eat grain, hay, grass, bread, carrots...in fact they'll eat anything you hand them, so you shouldn't ever give an elephant anything to play with like your hat or your shoes.

There are eighteen elephants and they're all females, because if you have males they'll fight to be the leader of the pack—and they'll fight for the girls. Elephants are very dangerous, especially males. If one goes wild, there's nothing you can do to stop him.

All of the elephants are from India except two from Africa. African elephants have bigger ears. And they're the ones with the tusks; even the girls have them.

My favorite elephants are Kongo and Pinky. I love to feed them. I just throw carrots into their mouths the same way I would pitch a baseball.

I like to visit the other animals too, and sometimes I feed the horses a little hay.

This year a baby camel was born. When a camel has only one hump it's called a dromedary. It will be about a year before he's old enough to join the show.

My brother Gino spends all the time he can visiting with the showgirls.

Poppy wishes he could spend *his* time visiting with the showgirls too, but he has to get in shape after the long train ride. A catcher's arms must be very strong, so my Dad works out lifting weights.

When we get to a new place, the performance director posts a schedule of our shows on a bulletin board backstage. We usually have two shows a day, one in the afternoon around four o'clock and another one in the evening at eight. On Saturdays we have *three* performances—at eleven, three, and eight! That's the day circus people really hate because we have to get up so early.

Since I can't go to regular school, I have to study with a tutor. Gino has the same tutor, but she usually works with us separately. Our school is in the mornings, starting at ten. It can't start any earlier because we don't get to bed until very late.

I like math and reading best. But I like playing even more, and that's what I always do as soon as I'm finished studying.

We don't have to be in the circus building until an hour before show time, but I usually go over earlier to see if anything's happening. Sometimes it's pretty quiet, so I just make up games that I can play by myself.

Other times I visit with my friends, especially Oliver Gebel-Williams and Michael, the candy man. Oliver and I like to pretend we're tightrope walkers. We also fool around on the ring curb.

Michael spins cotton candy, and I can usually count on him for a sample. Some is pink. Some is blue. Once he mixed the two colors and it came out purple. Yeech! It gets in my hair if I stand too close.

I wish I could play all the time before the show, but every so often I have certain responsibilities. My Dad says responsibilities are the difference between being a professional and being an amateur.

Once in a while I have to be interviewed for magazines and newspapers and have to pose for photographers. When they ask me how long I've been flying, I like to tell them that I went up before I was born. It's true, because Mama was flying while she was pregnant with me.

Every Friday before the show I stand in line for my paycheck. I get to keep ten dollars a week, and my Dad puts the rest into my savings account.

I also have to answer my fan mail.

The clowns are the first performers to arrive backstage. They have to start getting ready before anyone else because it takes them about an hour to put on their make-up. And they have to go in the ring twenty minutes before show time and perform for the people who turn up early. It's called the clown come-in.

Jim and I have been buddies for a long time. He's a "white face" or "picture" clown, which means he doesn't fall down or get slapped or have pies thrown at him.

He begins by covering his whole face with white paint. Then he covers it with Johnson's baby powder. Next he adds red, then he adds more powder, and then he puts on the black. He lets me do the final powder job.

Each clown has to do his own face, and Jim says you don't really get your face down until you've been in the show about a year.

He taught me a barrel gag.

There are twenty-nine clowns, and three of them are girls. The place where they hang out is called Clown Alley. I have the best time messing around with them.

When I hear the music for the clown come-in, I know I'd better get to my dressing room fast and get ready for the opening production number.

I have to wear rouge on my cheeks because the spotlights make everyone look so pale.

The ringmaster blows his whistle and the show begins. He always says the same thing: "Ladies and Gentlemen...Children of all ages..."

There's an opening parade and everyone who's in the circus takes part. I don't have to do anything until Spec, which is just before the intermission, so I usually watch part of the show. Gunther goes first and works in a big wire-mesh cage.

The clowns perform between the different acts. Frosty Little is Boss Clown. That means he's in charge of all the other clowns. He has to make sure that they're funny.

Lou Jacobs is the most famous clown in the world—he's been with the circus for almost sixty years. I love it when he pretends he's a mommy out for a stroll with a screaming baby.

Then Dolly Jacobs does a wonderful aerial routine on the roman rings. She's Lou Jacobs' daughter and a good friend of our family. Poppy is teaching her to fly.

I also like the Polish swing act—especially the part where one of the men jumps off his swing and gets hurled 30 feet high through a ring of fire.

The elephants always try to steal the show—and sometimes they do.

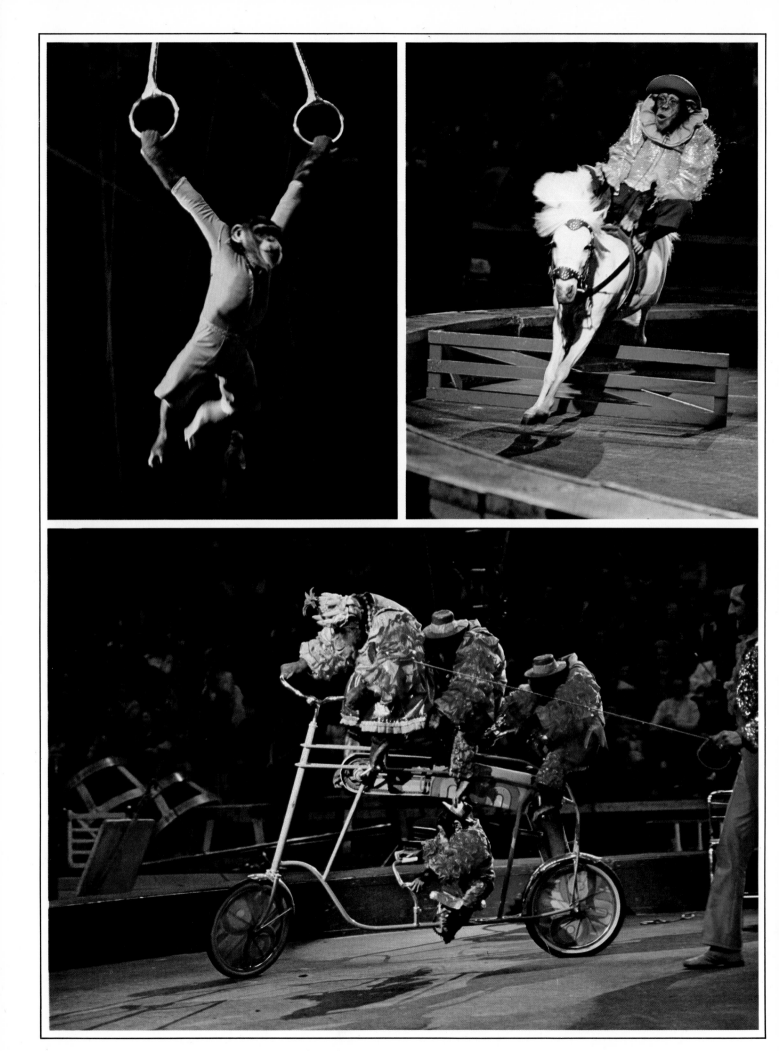

The chimps are *totally* crazy.

So is Pedro Carrillo on the highwire. It makes me *very* nervous to watch him, because he doesn't use a net. Last year his partner fell and hurt himself so badly that he can't perform any more. Now Pedro has another partner.

Mom does her dog act and I always watch that.

Then all twenty-eight showgirls perform an aerial ballet on the web. The men who stand below are called web-setters. Web is one of the prettiest acts in the circus.

At the end of the first half, we're all in the big Spectacle. Mama rides her elephant.

And I walk around the track waving to the audience. Then comes intermission.

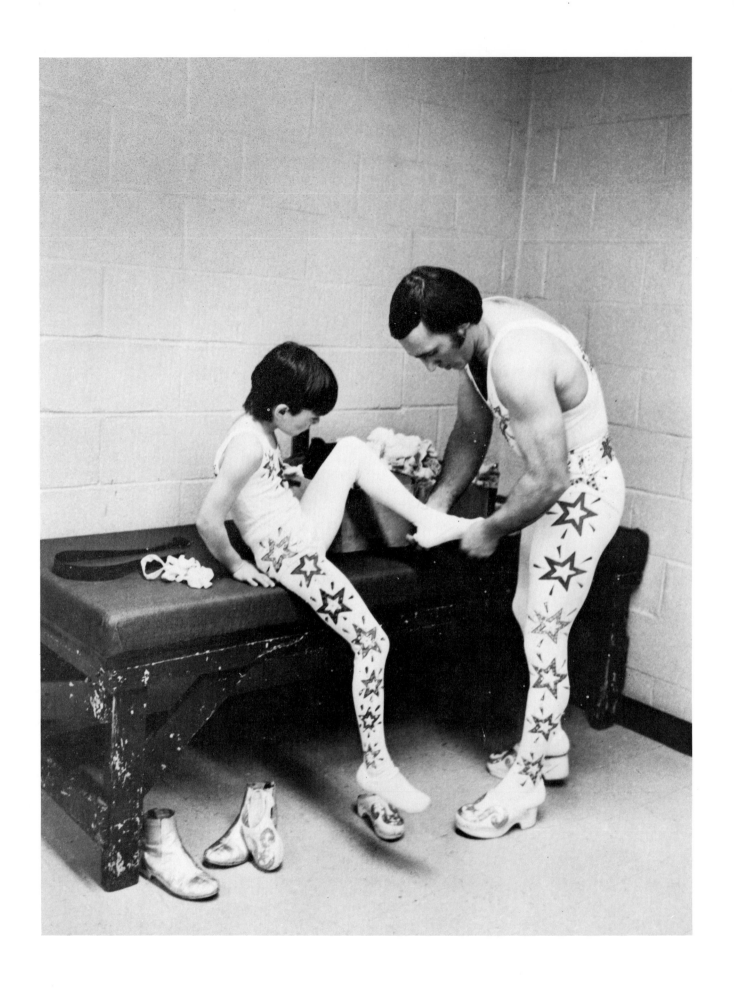

After intermission we start getting ready to fly. First we decide which set of tights to wear so we'll all match.

As soon as I'm dressed, Mama gives me a blast of hair spray.

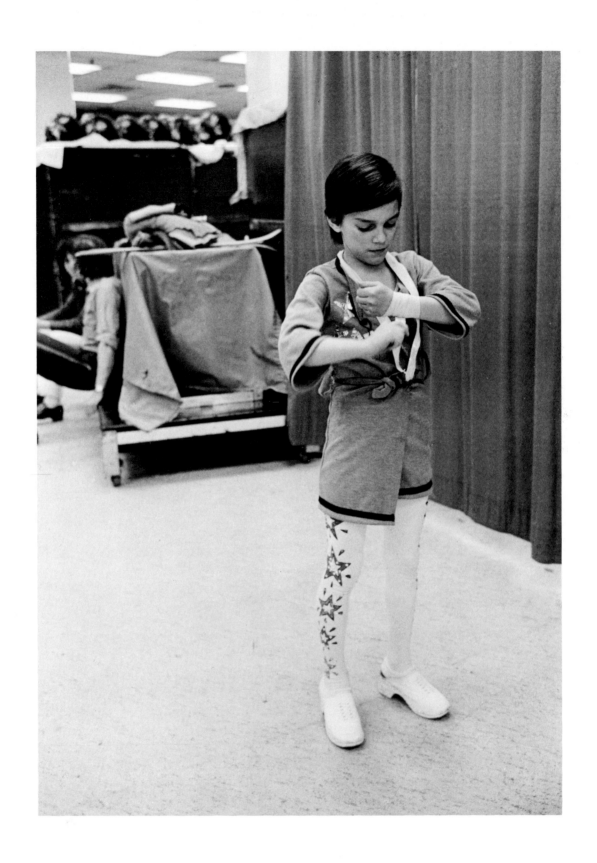

Then I put on my wrist bandages. I try to make the knots as little as possible
Big knots sometimes hurt when Poppy catches me.

We warm up for about twenty minutes on a bar outside our dressing room.

After we're warmed up, we put resin on our hands. That makes them sticky so we can get a good grip on the bar. Then my Dad puts alcohol on our bandages to prevent them from slipping. The temperature up in the air is different than it is on the ground. It's always much hotter up there.

Finally we do exercises to loosen up our shoulder muscles. Mom makes sure her crown is secure. My Dad checks my wrist bands to be certain I've done them right.

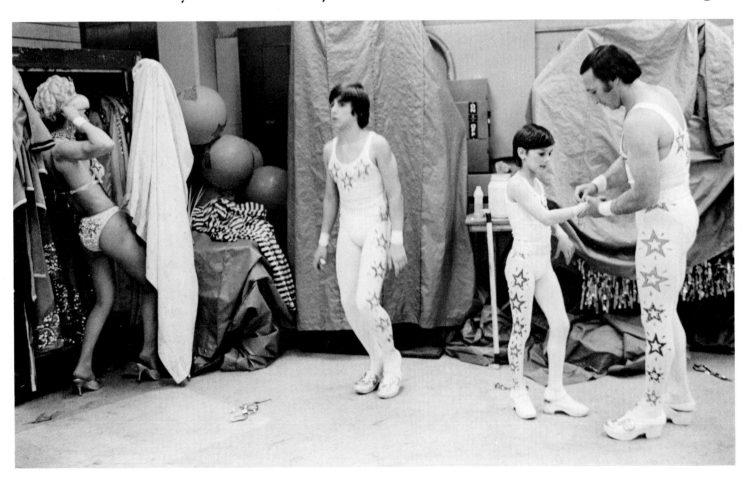

We can't put on our own capes because our hands are too sticky, so our cape man does it for us. We have three different sets of capes—blue, red, and shocking pink.

I love swirling my cape almost as much as I love flying.

Poppy gives us last-minute instructions and reminds me to open my hands for a quick grab. Then he kisses me and wishes me good luck.

When we have an early show, it's very hard to be alert. But as soon as I'm up there, I'm wide awake.

I always pray that I'll catch my trick and do it right, and that I won't get hurt. And I pray that Gino and my Mom will catch their tricks too. We all cross ourselves just before the spotlights hit us.

The ringmaster introduces us as we make our entrance. He says: "And now, in Ring 3—from Chile, the world-renowned 'Oscar' winners—the Flying Farfans!" Our cape man takes the capes after we've bowed, and then Mom, Gino, and I climb up a ladder to the platform. My Dad goes up his own ladder and gets on his catch bar.

People think you're scared if you don't smile. But you have to do it without taking your mind off the trick.

Mama goes first and does a full twisting somersault. Then Gino does a double layout. Then Mama goes again and does a double tuck somersault.

Mama and Gino do a spectacular trick where they pass each other in mid-air.

Then I go.

When I'm up in the air, I think I can do anything.

It really gives me a good feeling when people are watching me

One of the tricks I do is called hocks off. When Poppy says "Hup," I jump off the platform and swing, holding on to the bar with my hands. While I'm swing-ing, I put my legs up over the bar and let go with my hands. Then on my next swing I reach for my Dad, grab his wrists, and let go of the bar with my legs.

An "angel" is when I let go of one of his hands and he grabs my feet with his free hand. Then, when the bar returns, my Dad lets go of my feet and I fly.

When we're finished flying, we drop into the net, one by one, doing tricks on the way down. I throw a double.

When you fall into the net, you have to do it a certain way or you can really hurt yourself. You try to land flat on your back, in the center of the net. If you land on your seat, the bounce is too high. The first bounce is the one you must learn to control. You have to be sure not to grab the net, because it will cut your fingers. It could even break them.

Then I take my bow and say thank you to the audience. But when I've goofed up, it's hard to take the thank you. It makes me feel like a fool to ask for applause for something that wasn't well done.

Ours is the very last act in the show, so we just run backstage and grab our capes

We join the Finale, take one more bow, and the show is over.

Then we go back to our dressing room. If Gino and I have performed well, Poppy gets so excited. He jumps up and down and hugs us, and says how proud he is of his two sons.

Sometimes people come backstage to visit us. One night Amy Carter, the President's daughter, asked me for my autograph. Another time Princess Grace came to visit, because we had met her when we performed in Monaco. She couldn't believe that Gino was doing a triple somersault in performance.

We usually stay on for about two hours after the evening performance and work on our acts for the next year. That's the only time my Mom has to train the Dobermans, and we all try to help her.

The hardest part was getting the dogs to run through the fire. Gino and I ran through it first to convince them that there was nothing to it. They weren't very convinced.

It takes forever to teach a dog how to ride a motorcycle. My Dad made a set of training wheels for the bike. Now Chico has such a good time tooling around the ring that it's all we can do to get him to stop.

We're also working on a new flying act. Next year my cousin Kathy will probably go up with us. She just turned five.

After we're through rehearsing, we feed the dogs. Then we go back to the train and have dinner. Even though it's very late, we still need to unwind at the end of the day.

At last it's time to go to bed.

My friends ask me if I ever dream I'm a bird or Superman. Sometimes I do. But I'd rather be me — in the circus.

# Acknowledgments

As usual, there are lots of people to thank. Everyone at Ringling Bros. and Barnum & Bailey was wonderful to me—the performers out front and all the people who work so hard behind the scenes. I am especially grateful to producers Irvin and Kenneth Feld, who gave me access in the first place and who also went over the text and layout with me. June Forsythe, Nini Finkelstein, and Michael Burke were especially helpful and nice. Other stalwarts...June Makela, Sarah Carr, Kurt Vonnegut, Bob Gottlieb and the entire gang at Knopf.

And of course I couldn't have done this book without the Farfans. What an admirable family—and how proud I am to know them.

—Jill Krementz

## A Note About the Author

Jill Krementz is a well-known photographer of literary figures, a documentary photographer, and an author. Her pictures can be seen regularly in the *New York Times, New York* magazine, *People, Newsweek,* and other major periodicals, and she has photographs in the permanent collection of the Museum of Modern Art. Her previous books include *A Very Young Dancer, A Very Young Rider,* and *A Very Young Gymnast.* Recently she was chosen to take the official portraits of four members of the United States Cabinet.

## A Note on the Type

This book was set in a film version of Bulmer, a distinguished typeface long famous in the history of English printing, which was designed and cut by William Martin in about 1790 for William Bulmer of the Shakespeare Press. In design, it is all but a modern face, with vertical stress, sharp differentiation between the thick and thin strokes, and nearly flat serifs. The italic is taken from a font of Baskerville; Martin was John Baskerville's pupil.

The text was composed by Quad Typographers, Inc., New York, New York. The book was printed by Halliday Lithographers, West Hanover, Massachusetts, and bound by American Book–Stratford Press, Saddle Brook, New Jersey. Color engravings were made by Offset Separations, New York City; color lithography by Einsen Freeman Graphics, Fair Lawn, New Jersey.

Graphics were directed by R. D. Scudellari; book design and layout by Elissa Ichiyasu.